Taking Strikes:

Lessons Learned from Systema

Taking Strikes: Lessons Learned from Systema

by

Members of the

Central Florida Systema School

Foreword
Bob Elder Sensei

Active Wellness Press

Taking Strikes:
Lessons Learned from Systema

by

Members of the
Central Florida Systema School

Published by
Active Wellness Press
Orlando, FL USA

Orders: CFLSystema.wordpress.com

All rights reserved. No part of this book may be reproduced or transmitted in any form or by any means, electronic or mechanical, including photocopying, recording or by any information storage and retrieval system, without written permission from the publisher and author(s), except for the inclusion of brief quotations in a review.

Copyright ©2012 by David Orman, Instructor, CFL Systema.

ISBN-13: 978-1478399957

First Edition.

Dedications

As a School, we humbly dedicate this book to a great teacher, brilliant martial artist and model for us to follow . . . . . . Vladimir Vasiliev.

Because of your willingness to share this wonderful art, our lives have been greatly enhanced.

I would like to dedicate this book also to David and Rick Merrell. Because of your selflessness, dedication and patience with Systema, my skills have improved and more so, my life has become much better. I will forever be grateful.

Also to my wife, Lisa. Thank you for your patience, support and tolerance in this great adventure of Systema.   *--David Orman*

I would like to dedicate my chapter to my late grandmother Dolores "Nana" Moses who was fascinated with Russia and its culture and would have been equally fascinated with my new endeavor.   --Thomas Moses

I would like to thank my wife Janet, my parents Paul and Barbara Warcholak, my first martial arts instructor Dave Majic, my current instructor David Orman and our entire group at Central Florida Systema. --*Jon Warcholak*

I would like to dedicate my chapter to my wife Lynn without her love and support I wouldn't be able to pursue all of my dreams and wishes.

I Love You baby.   --*Edward Wiatrowski*

Dedicated to my wife Judy, and my sons Randy and Jimmy, all of whom have put up with my craziness for decades. - *Jim Hampshire*

Foreword

by

Bob Elder Sensei

I have been involved with martial arts for over 39 years to date. I started with Isshin Ryu karate and for more than 2 decades, have been focusing on Japanese sword now (Toyama Ryu). I have visited Japan frequently and have had the great honor of training with some of the best martial artists in the entire world.

Under the tutelage of Hataya Yoshitoki Sensei, I both study and teach a modern version of Toyama Ryu for the last 22 years. I am the founder and Kaicho of Zen Nihon Toyama Ryu Iaido and founded the first American version of Zen Nohon Batto Do Renmei.

In addition, I have owned and operated East Coast Martial Arts Supply Store for 33 years. During this time, I have come across virtually every martial art known. I have also seen countless martial artists, both students and instructors come through my doors, all of whom covered a wide spectrum of skill, talent, experience and ability.

A year ago, I called David Orman to see if he would be interested in teaching me Systema, on a one-on-one basis. I thought I might like this art and decided to give it a try. One of my employees started taking lessons and raved about it.

I find it completely fascinating and enlightening. It has added to my martial arts in many, unique ways. The most important way has been the awareness of a new version of fighting art that was previously unknown to me. It has opened new doors to an incredible amount of possibilities. New thought. New actions!

I have pursued a "Way" through Iai and now feel as if I have broken free of rigid kata bunkai and expanded my thought processes of development. It is like coming up from the bottom of a well and seeing the sky.

Systema is now a part of my regular training. I am thankful to have access to an Instructor here in Orlando.

If you have been studying this art, you can certainly relate. If you have not yet had the pleasure of experiencing it, your current art and your overall life will improve.

Bob Elder
Chief Instructor, Toyama Ryu Iaido

Introduction

Take a handful of people and ask them about their experiences in Systema, and you will have a handful of vastly different stories.

That is what this book is about. A vastly different group of men and women – some with extensive martial arts training and others with none – who have come together over the years and become part of Central Florida Systema school.

These are our stories.

This book is not about instructions or a "how to learn Systema" manual. Any martial artist worth their salt knows you cannot learn an art from a book or DVD. This book is about the personal side to this incredible art.

It is our hope that by reading our stories, you will be inspired to train, motivated to train harder and experience fully what Systema has to offer.

Some people train for protection. Others train because their job demands it. Most of us train for far different reasons.

We are not police officers or SWAT team members. We do not have extensive histories of physical conflict. No one will be joining the

UFC anytime soon. We are parents, Internet business owners, salespeople, runners and of course, Systema practitioners. We want to learn this art because we love it.

We also have a secret to share and it is this: We train to become better people. We do not leave our daily problems outside the school door. We bring it with us and by working with Systema and the energy, we work out our problems.

We do not always know how this works – only that it works.

It is the ultimate win/win. We get to train and become more physically fit. We get to train and become better people.

And oh by the way, defending ourselves and our family is not a problem either.

These are our stories. We hope they are inspirational to read as they were to experience.

One last suggestion. . . .

Join our class and **Create your own experiences.**

Hitting the Right Note

by

Jon Warcholak

I have always thought of myself as a laid-back person. I was not a person for whom anxiety or nervousness was an issue. Certainly not a person for whom stress would cause any physical, mental or emotional problems. Several years ago I began to notice these types of stresses creeping into my life. Maybe they had been present for a while and I had simply failed to notice them.

While living near a large city for the first time, I found myself becoming furious with traffic, both with the other drivers as well as with the flow of vehicles and even with the designs of the roads. I recall one occasion in which I furiously pounded on the steering wheel and shouted at the…. well, traffic. My traveling companion was not impressed. I was stressing about work or lack thereof. I was working a day job and freelancing as a musician at the time. I was barely scraping by financially and my career was not going the way I had hoped.

I had not really connected these two situations, nor the other half forgotten negativity in my life at the time. But, I soon began to feel unwell. Headaches, lack of energy and even occasional dizziness. My doctor advised me that I was probably experiencing anxiety brought on by stress and some poor dietary choices. She said to try to relax, cut out fatty foods and caffeine, get some exercise and reduce the factors causing stress in my life.

Surprise! I couldn't believe it. I was only in my mid twenties and I didn't even have a high stress job or home life. But I wanted to feel better, so I did what the doctor suggested. I didn't feel like I could do much about the external causes. I cut out caffeine, quit fast food, exercised more. I even began taking karate classes again. It was a different style than the Shorin-Ryu that I studied as a kid, but it was close. (For those wondering if this is the part about Systema, the answer is: not yet). I started to feel much better and life took me on my way.

Things were going well shortly after that time. I was doing what I loved: playing music for a living on-board a cruise ship. I was meeting new people and had fairly stress free lifestyle. It was only very occasionally, every year or two, that I would feel those same symptoms creeping back into my life. Increased headaches, lack of energy and pretty infrequent dizzy spells. The dizziness was always the one to make me take step back and modify my behavior. Often I would rhetorically ask myself, "What do I have to be stressed or anxious about?"

A few more years passed and I have continued my life back on land. I'm finally making more money doing what I love. My wife and I had been in our first home for a few years. I had a bit of stress in my life, but I handled it well. Only occasionally, I felt those stress symptoms try to creep up on me, but I would reduce them the same way each time with exercise and better diet.

I tend to operate in cycles in terms of fitness and health. In hindsight, my buildups of anxiety are probably part of the cycle. Eat healthy and exercise for a while, slowly fade out of that back into bad habits, start feeling bad, restart cycle. About four months prior to this writing, I was looking for something different to do physically. I had done a lot of different activities over the years from simple walking to karate, weight training to yoga and too many others to mention here. I had been receiving the quarterly catalog for activities at my local community center for about two years. Each time I browsed through, I saw something called Systema listed as the only martial arts offering. It sounded interesting, but not really what I was accustomed to in terms of martial arts training. The "special forces" description was not really appealing to me. I was imagined a style that was *more* rigid than my experiences with karate. But I decided to give it a try anyway since the class was held only a couple miles from my house.

On the surface, what I found at the class was somewhat unremarkable: a medium sized, friendly group of people learning together from and with a personable instructor. I must admit I was a little disappointed that I could not make use of my old gi, but the informal atmosphere was a refreshing difference from my past experiences.

After a brief warmup, we were immediately working in pairs or groups. This was the first big difference: no standing in place punching or kicking the air. We were immediately executing defense/attack scenarios with a partner. Much to my surprise and delight, beyond the fundamental actions, creativity was even *encouraged!* Obviously this was not an art of clones, but one of uniqueness. As much as I enjoyed that first class, I had only a glimpse the underlying concepts that would become beneficial to me outside of Systema as well.

I do not recall whether it was the second class or later, but I distinctly remember the first time I was made aware of my tension by my instructor. I do not remember the incident in detail as much as I remember my feelings and thoughts at the time. We were working with a partner on a series of techniques with which I thought I was doing pretty well. David, my instructor, was making his way around to help each group. When he came over to observe us, he lightly tapped my shoulders and said, "Relax." After my initial surprise, my instinct was to respond to the contrary. I *thought* I felt very relaxed, more than usual in fact. Fortunately, I kept it to myself as I looked inward and realized that he was right.

During the following days, I became mindful of my levels of tension more often. It almost became a game for me to check myself during all sorts of different activities. Walking the dog was the strangest to me, since I noticed frequent tension in myself, regardless of the dog's behavior. However, the most important aspect of recognizing this tension for me was while playing music.

Although I was very new to Systema and had practiced some other martial arts on and off for a total of around nine years, I had been involved in playing and performing music consistently for thirty. It was something I did (and still do) everyday. I am fortunate that it is my job and my hobby. I work very hard at it and enjoy doing it. That being said, it is the activity where I noticed the most tension in myself.

As I became more adept at recognizing and reconciling this tension at class each week while I practiced Systema, I applied the techniques to my musical endeavors. What a difference! It was difficult at first, but I soon found myself breathing with the music like I breathed with physical movements in class. I was more mentally relaxed during performances with less tension in my arms and fingers. I was able to pull of more difficult musical passages while *trying less.* I had read about these types of musical experiences for years, but this was this first time I really felt it.

I soon found myself practicing breathing and relaxation during all sorts of activities: Driving, cooking, walking the dog of course, and even during conversations. By simply focusing on the tension in my body, then releasing it with breath tied to movement or activity (it works with mental activity too), I have been able to reduce stress and focus more easily at any task at hand.

In addition to helping make life generally more enjoyable and healthful, I have experienced some unexpected benefits. When I am truly able to function in this zone of relaxation, which is not nearly all the time, but more than one might think, my level of energy increases. Consequently, I am able to get a lot more done in any given time period. I have even been able to reduce my daily caffeine intake from half a pot of coffee a day down to one green tea on most days and sometimes none. This relaxed, focused state of mind seems to increase efficiency and limit frustration as well.

In my search for a new physical activity to try,

I found an art in Systema which has profoundly impacted all aspects of my life for the better. I am indebted to the founders and my instructor and I look forward to passing on what I have learned. My favorite part is that I am just getting started.

Going Out of Your Way

by

David Orman

I have seen or heard about it so often that I now consider it a silent but powerful part of martial arts.

My friend, *Bob Elder Sensei* spoke about the challenges and difficulties he overcame when training in Japan. The teaching was not easily accessible but he found a way to consistently train with dedicated efforts.

My Systema teacher, David Merrell talks about how there were no teachers in W. Palm Beach (or anywhere else in Florida at the time) and as such, had to travel to Russia and Toronto when he was starting out in this art.

I watch my wife Lisa overcome some struggles of the past 3 years to finally get things moving with the art of Kyudo. A 14 hour trip to Pensacola was one example.

My own experience in *Systema* is a similar story — November will be my 50th trip to W.

Palm to train, as there are no other teachers in my area.

Each of the aforementioned have a clear theme — A strong desire to learn and the willingness to go out of your way. It is as if the Universe is posing a a one-question test. *"How badly do you want it?"*

She really does not care, nor even listen to your verbal answer. She only observes your behavior. The Universe is too intelligent to be fooled by words.

Over time, it does not get easier. I still travel 6 hours every month to train on the blacktop, complete with glass, nails and heat. The distance has not been magically shortened.

Elder Sensei consistently had to overcome the biases that existed in the world of Iaido. No excuses. Just dedication.

David Merrell never received any free trips to Moscow.

Though the details never change, there is a huge shift internally. The rewards of going out of your way for years and years begin to mean something to the individual. The feeling of accomplishment(s) have deeper meaning because so much additional effort had to be made.

Somehow the wine tastes a little sweeter.

I notice this in my classes as well. One student is a medical doctor who has his practice an hour away. He never misses class. One has a high stress management job, along with a very young daughter. He has missed a grand total of one class in 5 months.

Regardless of obstacles, some find a way around, under or through them. They go out of their way.

The training is not any easier for such individuals. Mistakes are common. Frustration comes for frequent visits. The big difference is that such individuals treat their training off the mats the same as they do on the mats. Their martial art never stops just because they are not in class or wearing a Systema shirt.

Learning to overcome obstacles and go out of your way is just as important to a martial artist as defending against a front kick or getting out of a headlock. The little things matter.

In fact, at some point we realize the little things are really the big things that made the difference.

Like going out of your way.

My Journey

by

Michael Carrasquilla

Ralph Waldo Emerson once wrote "Life is a journey, not a destination." As for life, so too these words are true for the Martial Arts. It is a path of struggle and sweat, of growth and accomplishment, and, as in life, no two travelers paths will be the same.

My journey began with Saturday afternoon Kung-Fu Theater. Movies like Return of the 36th Chamber, Fist of the White Lotus and Shaolin Master Killer introduced me to a whole new world and sparked a love for the Martial Arts. It was like magic, skilled warriors fighting scores of enemies, flying through the air with a grace and ferocity. I thought to myself this is what I want, I want to know what they know, do what they do. All great journeys begin with a thought and a simple step. I had my thought; all I needed was the step.

My first formal martial art was Tae Kwon Do, a Korean martial art most known for its emphasis on kicking techniques. Growing up in the Bronx, it should be little surprise that my instructors also put a very strong emphasis in the practical self-defense aspects of Tae Kwon Do and incorporated many precepts of boxing. Kicks like the Axe Kick, Tornado Kick and the Jumping Spinning Hook Kick invoked memories of Kung-Fu Theater.

Sparring matches typically began with padding clad opponents four to five feet apart; a distance usually maintained given the leg is the longest natural weapon available to a martial artist.

There were long, hard hours spent doing push-ups, sit-ups and jumping jacks; practicing technique after technique twenty to thirty times in a row, sweat, sore muscles and the sheer exhilaration of "getting it." Struggling to learn a kick then seeing it fly off as naturally as breathing makes every drop of sweat, and occasionally blood, worth it.

I spent the next few years continuing my study of Tae Kwon Do even being privileged to teach it, to pass on what I had learned. In teaching, I believe I gained my greatest appreciation for Martial Arts and began to feel that there must be more. That despite all that I had gleaned thus far from Tae Kwon Do these were still my first steps and that I had not yet found the ultimate "Way."

The next leg of my journey would take me to the halls of Wah Lum Kung-Fu. Chinese martial arts are classically categorized as either Northern or Southern styles. Northern styles generally emphasize long range techniques, wide stances and employee a greater number of kicks than their Southern counterparts. It was an almost natural progressive fit for someone from a predominately kicking art.

One of the biggest hurdles I had to overcome was that sparring was now a much closer affair. Where in Tae Kwon Do opponents where around five feet apart, Kung-Fu opponents where at arm's length away (around two feet or closer). Even though Northern Styles employ more kicks; kicks in traditional Kung-Fu systems rarely raise above the mid-section. The majority of techniques are focused on the upper body weapons, such as the hands, forearms and elbows. It was through this Praying Mantis form of Kung-Fu that I was introduced grappling, or Chin Na in Chinese. Arm bars, wrist and joint locks were now added to my repertoire. Each new technique was a discovery, an expansion of my mind and my perception like learning new words expands one's vocabulary. It was in this art that I also received my first formal training in weapons.

For just about anyone, the correlation between armed and unarmed combat is a no-brainer. Weapons have distinctive and, in most cases, deadly advantages but there is a huge difference from academically understanding the importance of weapons and holding one in your hands. It is that reason that I believe Weapons' training is a must in any martial system. Training with weapons forces a martial artist to move and even think differently. The weight, length, lethality of weapons effects movement, body position and even strategy. Whether you want it to or not, weapons are game changers. Try wielding a Guan Dao, Naginata or even a simple Bo Staff and you'll see what I mean.

Weapons' training enhances a martial artist's unarmed techniques as well. I feel in many cases that properly employing a technique, whether it be defensive or offensive, with a weapon forces a practitioner to have even better body mechanics than is usually needed without using a weapon. A lesson gleamed from the next leg of my journey, a Japanese Martial Art called Bujinkan.

Bujinkan, or know formally as *Bujinkan Budō Taijutsu,* is closely associated with Ninjutsu and consists of nine separate ryũha or schools. My experience and knowledge of throws, holds, and joint locks that was obtained from Kung-Fu flowed with my new art gracefully.

Two new insights that I was introduced to were the use of proper body movement and positioning as opposed to strength to defeat an opponent and the use of precise strikes to pressure and nerve points. At this point of my journey Bujinkan would become the most intense art that I had studied.

The art focuses on combat and as such gone were the Poomses (Forms or Katas) of Tae Kwon Do and in was the concept of "feeling" a move or technique. To understand what it can do to your opponent you must first experience it. Coming home after training with bruises on my neck, arms and legs were common place. Each class was direct application and would teach that every move has a counter if you can learn to adapt to the "flow" of a situation.

What seems simple now was the eye opening lesson that body movement alone could provide protection and generate large amounts of energy. Stepping at a 45 degree angle or shifting my weight to one side could easily move me out of my opponents range but still leave me in a position to attack. Despite the pain and hard work there is a part of me that loves training and what kid that grew up on Kung-Fu Theater wouldn't relish at the idea of studying Ninjutsu?

For a time, Life would have new challenges for me;

such as starting a family and as so the martial arts would fade to my past but always a part of me. As inevitable as the rising sun (and as corny as that sounds) I would return training and to Kung-Fu.

This part of my journey would once again introduce me to an entirely new understanding of martial arts in general; the concept of Hard and Soft (or External and Internal) martial arts. "Hard and soft" refers to how forcefully a martial artist counters the force of an attack. Hard techniques or styles meet a force with force.

Like in Karate or Tae Kwon Do blocking or striking rely complete on muscle and are intended to break an opponent or halt an attack. Soft (or Internal) styles aim to turn an attacker's force to the advantage of the practitioner. By applying proper body movement and flow an attacker's force can be redirected with minimal effort and can lead to devastating counter attacks. In this aspect Bujinkan was my actual first experience with Internal Styles but it wasn't until through my new instructor who taught very classic Internal Chinese Styles such as Wing Chun, Baguazhang and Hsing-I that I really began to understand. Another concept that I learned, that was a favorite of my new instructor, was that of Raison D'etre. Raison D'etre is French for "reason for existence."

My instructor's belief was that every technique had a purpose, some were obvious but many were hidden. He like my Bujinkan instructor believed that the key to everything was in the details but that it was important to not get lost in them. Through use of proper body movement an opponent can be defeated with little to no effort, but the demand of proper body movement means the subtle difference of where you step or shifting your weight at the right time can mean the difference between success or "getting your head caved in."

It also means that becoming too focused on the step or the weight shift can lead to ignoring flow and consequently "getting you head caved in". It was through the idea of Raison D'etre that I learned to break down and analyze a technique and began to truly appreciate the philosophical aspects of the martial arts. The written works of Sun Tzu, Miyamato Musashi and of course Bruce Lee; had new meaning and insight for me.

I am a Bruce Lee fan, as I'm sure many martial artists are, but it wasn't until later in my life that I truly had an appreciation for his philosophy on martial arts and life. Early on I was seeking an ultimate "Way," as I think many of us all do, and it's around this time that an inscription he made for his wife opened my eyes. He inscribed "Using no way as way, having no limitation as limitation". It had connected all that I had learned to show me that systems were the beginning not the end, that each "Way" that I studied was bringing me to an understanding of myself. Something that I believe is a universal truth.

Musashi once wrote "You must understand that there is more than one path to the top of the mountain". I see my progression through the arts has a clear and straight line to art that I study now. Systema is an art that can be as varied and unique as each practitioner that embraces it.

"Adapt what is useful, reject what is useless, and add what is specifically your own." Bruce Lee wrote those words and I believe they are the heart of what Systema is. Systema is an adaptable, flowing art and is yet powerful and forceful at the same time. I see it as an art that connects to me at the core of who and what I am. It challenges me physically and mentally, it has forced me to faces my fears of being hit and pushed my understanding of mind over body. Even though I am still at my infancy with Systema I see how it connects and advances everything I have learned up to this point and feel privileged to be part of it.

My thanks to Vladimir Vasiliev and Michael Ryabko; and especially to my instructor David Orman and all my brothers and sisters in Systema and good luck on your journey.

"The journey is what brings us happiness not the destination"   -Dan Millman

Opening up the World

by

Carlos Alvarado

How I found Systema?

I have been attracted to martial arts since I saw the first Bruce Lee movie. It took me many years later to sign up for Tae kwon do. I practiced the style for 2 years before moving to Florida in 1987. Life got in the way (that is my excuse) and I never got around practicing any martial arts until 2011 when I found a meet up group (Orlando's Martial Arts Meetup Group) that would bring instructors from the different martial arts every Sunday.

It was on one of those meetup about Dim Mak that I met David Orman, Central Florida Systema Instructor and Garth Widdows, a student at Central Florida Systema School. During our conversation I mentioned that I come to the meetup but I do not practice any particular martial art. David replied "Not yet" and he smiled. At the end of the meetup I asked David for information about the school location. I was intrigued to find out what Systema was about and decided I was going home to investigate (technical word for google it) and find more Systema.

After watching a few videos, my interest continue growing. I looked up the address of the school but was disappointed to find out it was too far from my home; I lived on the other side of town. I found myself finding another excuse to not participate. However, after a while I decided to make the drive and try one class. A I was driving to class on a Monday evening and paying tolls, I kept thinking about the distance, the miles, and the price of gas. I simply was not sure this was for me. I got to class and found a group of very friendly people; the training began, and I felt this group wanted people to individually learn but also wanted everyone to learn. This cohesive group and the training for that day made a big difference, and all the excuses (tolls, gas, and driving distance) were out the window. I made the decision at the end of the class that this was what I wanted to do. I got hooked on Systema.   Now when my friends ask how did you find Systema , my answer is "Systema found me."

Why Systema is good for me?

Training in Systema benefits my life outside of class. During my younger years I was a very good student and was very motivated to accomplish my goals. I graduated from high school at 16 and a started a bachelor degree in engineering. I completed a 5 year degree (169 semester credits) in 4 ½ years. At that age I thought I could accomplish anything and I was able to set goals and priorities without any distractions.

Once I started working and did not move in my career as I thought I would, I got complacent. I enjoyed my life and tried to work hard and play hard but I felt I was not living life to the fullest; there was something missing and I did not know what it was. I was still reluctant to try new activities, and fear paralyzed me - fear of failure.

Practicing Systema has helped me to overcome the fear of "not doing things right" because it is the trying that counts, and not the end results. I now realize that I have to try new things just for the experience without expecting to master anything but mastering having fun. This new way of thinking is motivating me to try new things such as learning Brazilian Portuguese, target practice with handguns, skeet shooting, and many other things that I keep adding to my bucket list.

My Systema instructor, David Orman, says to take the brain out and write the following 4 important things you need to know: breathing, structure, relaxation, and movement. Those actions are so powerful (you would think it is easy to do) and they are fundamentals to Systema that would help you not only to be better at Systema but to improve your life. Breathing clears you mind, release tension which result in relaxation and efficient movement.

I am now aware of tension in my all activities outside training. I find myself applying those principles in work and family situations allowing me to think clearly, articulate my ideas better and become a better contributor at work, and a better husband and father.

Shifting Focus

by

Carlos Guzman

Ever since I saw my first Systema DVD, I wanted a teaching certificate in this art! I loved it that much. That's what I had as a goal since I started training, followed by the process of making videos and sending them to Vladimir for evaluation. Funny how things change, the deeper you get into them.

The feedback from Vlad was specific, direct and to the point. I was to continue to work on the basics – breathing, relaxation, movement and structure, as well as move in a spontaneous fashion. It may not have been what I wanted to hear, but it was what I needed to hear.

So, it was back to the training floor, with corrections in mind and practice. Practice when I could, practice when I didn't really want to. Simply apply the valuable information and practice, practice and more practice.

Somewhere in between sessions, I would do more videos and send them over to headquarters for review. It became an exercise in determination, discipline and dedication. After all, I really wanted that certification.

Over time, a major shift occurred. I came to realize that I really wanted to do was EXPERIENCE Systema, in all its glory and entirely. This meant so much more than the certificate. It really spoke to me. It is my truth.

Shifting my focus to experiencing Systema rather then just "training" or following the instructions and adjusting the errors, has allowed me to let go of my ego. Also along the way, I dropped off the frustration of whether I am doing this right or not, the anxiety of getting reviewed by my peers and the focus of getting that certificate. In other words, I was becoming a better person through practicing this great art. Isn't that what this is all about anyway?!

Before, the "certification focus" was causing tension, the major obstacle in this art. My breathing was affected, my body and therefore my movements turned freedom of movement into a "technique," not true Systema.

Going forward in this art, I want to experience Systema – all of it. I want to apply the principles by living it, focusing on myself, my breath, my body, and my emotions.

The rest, I learned, will come naturally, becoming part of me, because Systema is part of me.

Characteristics of a Great Teacher
by
David Orman

I have had the good fortune of having some exceptional teachers currently and as part of my history. I also have had the fortune of having contrasting situations as a student. Each situation taught me a great deal and the contrast was itself, the ultimate teacher. Every time I have the opportunity to teach, I remind self what made my favorite teachers (like Vladimir and David Merrell) so valuable, and what made my *less-than-favorite* teachers so difficult. . . applying the former and avoiding the latter.

There are many characteristics that come to mind when thinking of some of the great teachers in my life. Passionate, skilled, ability to personalize instruction and drawing the best from students come to mind quickly.

A great teacher is brimming with energy and that passion is contagious. They continually light the fuse for themselves and serve as a model for others to follow. They never light the fuse FOR the student; rather, they point out the fuse and the matches. It is the student's responsible to mix the two.

Of course, their skill level is very high. Some of the very best teachers I have had were also some of the very best practitioners in the country. This however, is not always a pre requisite. Yes, skill is a must but sometimes, a great teacher was not always a great practitioner. Tommy Lasorda, the manager of the Los Angeles Dodgers comes to mind. Hall of Fame manager. Sub-par player. Some are blessed with the mind and the heart, but not always the body.

Everyone is built differently and the great teachers adjust to their students' physical and emotional makeup. Some love to be pushed hard. Others will crumble under such pressure. It does not make the former strong and the latter weak. It makes 2 people uniquely different. As such, they should be taught in much different fashions. A great teacher will see this quickly and adjust.

Drawing the best from each student was one of my favorite characteristics. My best teachers would put the goal (metaphorically speaking), an inch beyond my reach. It would dangle in front of me closely enough to serve as a huge motivator, yet just beyond, causing me to work hard and in a dedicated fashion toward it. Put things too close to the student and they lose interest. Make it too difficult and they lose heart. Correct distant is a tremendous key to outstanding teaching.

I think if there were characteristics that jumped out from the world of contrast it is these two:

1. Everyone want to be treated with respect and

2. Everyone wants to be Inspired.

Respect. *Do unto others. . . .*

Correct their actions. Make it about their action, not themselves. Most people are not professional athletes. They are doing this for fun, for self-growth and other personal factors. In my martial arts school, my students are not learning to be SWAT or special forces members. They are business people, mechanics and waiters. There is never a need to belittle, embarrass or correct in such a way that it affects their core.

Inspired. *What heights can you reach. . . .*

I have often said that the number one cause of disease – being it physical or emotional – is boredom. It has caused more illnesses, deaths and heartbreaks than all of the cancers combined. The cure is simple – Inspiration.

People want to be challenged. They want to release their Soul to soar like an eagle. Physical events or activities is a great method of accomplishing this. Doing pushups or defending a front kick may not change the world. It may change an individual's world though, with Inspiration serving as the driving force behind it.

Take care of these 2 and you have the makings of a booming school with happy students. Dismiss these and regardless of talent or pedigree, you will be one lonely teacher.

Flowing Through Life

by

Jim Hampshire

I started Systema looking for something to deal with problem drunks and addicts at fire and medical scenes as a firefighter. I have learned that, but I've also learned and used many more skills when I least expected it.

My previous martial arts training had me memorizing set-piece moves and then performing them on command with military precision and a loud "kihap." Unfortunately, it was worse than useless when I wound up in fights - I could destroy inanimate objects, but when I got jumped it didn't go well. I got hit numerous times trying to get into the proper fighting stance and encounters always seemed to deteriorate into brawls.

Two days of defensive tactics in medic school were a step in the right direction, but fell far short of what I was looking for.

Systema "clicked" with me right from the start. There were no unnecessary rituals or formalities, David was direct, friendly and got straight to the point. From day one he taught me exactly what I needed and didn't waste time with fluff. Systema seems complete, current, dynamic and natural. The breathing, balance and movement feel right, and seemed to be the key parts missing from my previous martial arts training. There was also something comforting about Systema. I can't put my finger on it, but going to class was the highpoint of my week while in medic school, helping to keep me centered and sane.

Unfortunately, as medic school intensified I drifted away from class – I simply ran out of hours in the day as I rotated between class, clinical time and work. By the time I finished I was in terrible physical shape, and Systema stayed on the back burner as I immersed myself in fitness training, getting back where I needed to be as a firefighter. But even though I had stopped training for a year, Systema was still there and influencing me.

In the Fire Academy, I had never been comfortable with breathing my air down until the mask sucked to my face. I spent time working on Systema breath exercises and when I did it in refresher training I found it easy to relax and control my breathing.

In mountain bike riding I became smoother and faster when I stopped forcing things and started flowing with the bike and trails. And in the back of my mind I drew the parallel with the movement and flow in class.

And then I had a high speed crash on a steep downhill in a mountain bike race. As I went over the handlebars I literally flashed back to jumping and rolling on bare tile in class. I tucked my chin, rolled across my back - right shoulder blade across to left hip - and slid to a stop. Though I was skinned and bruised, nothing was broken and I got up and finished the race. If I hadn't instantly rolled I'd have broken bone or been seriously injured.

Returning to the CFL Systema class was seamless. The details were rough, but the overall flow was still there. By the end of the first class I was back into the swing of things, and with a new appreciation of the art. Directing energy, maintaining balance, situational awareness - these are not only combat skills but, in a larger sense, life skills. Riding a motorcycle in traffic, making entry into a fire, clearing a pistol stage, moving through the woods - it all comes into play, only the details differ.

I haven't been in a fight since starting Systema, but the skills are there if needed. In the meantime I'll practice flowing through life

Finding the Self in a Push Up

by

Garth Widdows

My path to Systema began on May 9th 2011, my 33rd birthday, I had the day off from work and had spent the morning down at the lake fishing. While walking back to my house for lunch I stopped and picked up the mail. Inside was a brochure that the city put out every quarter listing the activities and events that would be taking place. As I sat at the table eating and thumbing through the brochure I came across a small snippet that read "Systema- The martial arts used by Spetsnaz." I read on and found out the the classes was held to the community center not far from my house and best of all, there was a class that night.

In my youth I studied Judo, Karate and Tae Kwon Do. I pursued Tae Kwon Do the furthest, stopping just short of testing for black belt. I always enjoyed the disciple of the martial arts. However, it was my Ta Kwon Do sensei who taught me to appreciate them for a different reason.

My Sensei used to say that martial arts were more about developing the self then learning self defense. I remember he once told me that learning to hit someone is no where near as important as learning to be calm when someone is trying to hit you. In our lives, unless you are a professional fighter, it is rare that we would raise our fist and punch someone. How many time a day however must we remain calm in stressful situations? And that is where the lesson lies, that is where one begins to develop the self. These lessons were not only the foundation of the martial arts but of life in general.

I began looking for for a new martial arts school in early 2011. I was shocked at what I found was out there. There were a few smaller schools in my area. The market however, seemed to be dominated by these larger "Belt Mills." The deep, self-developmental messages that I learned as a kid seemed to have been replaced by the concept that everything important is held in colored piece of cloth on your waist. I was consistently told that if I just signed a minimal two year contract, with the prior experience I have, I could have my black belt in little over a year.

I even had one instructor, after I told him was going home to think about enrolling in his school, stop me at the door and tell me he would start me as a brown belt if I signed the contract that day. Absolute absurdity. I had not taken a class in 15 years and he was ready to make me a brown belt. The rank was nothing more than a bargaining tool. It appeared as if I was never going to find what I was looking for - a school that would developed me both physically and mentally.

It was around four o'clock that Monday night when my wife asked me what I wanted for my birthday dinner. With the city flyer still in my hand I told her instead of dinner I would like to go try this class. My wife told me it was my birthday and I could do as I pleased just have fun and don't get hurt as I was now a "old man."

When I arrived at Systema class I could sense a

great vibe in the room. As people walked in everyone was smiling and embracing. There was a true sense of bonding.

The class began with some unique warm up exercises. We walked across people's stomachs as everyone was shoulder to shoulder on the ground. We preformed a squat while back to back with a partner. And we stood against the wall, in a squatting position while our partner stood on our thighs. All of there exercises not only prepared us physically for what was ahead in class but they also prepared us mentally, to over come discomfort and fear. This lesson would also be taught at the end of class.

With ten minutes left David, our instructor, said that we would now be performing strikes. Strikes are the practice of delivering and taking punches. I watched as student after student line up, stood next to David, focused their breathing, then took a devastating punch to the stomach. Again this lesson was not only to teach you what it was like to get hit in the stomach, it was also to teach you how to overcome your fear. Finally I had found what I was looking for.

I spent the rest of that night at home researching as much as I could about Systema. I learned how it was developed in Russia after centuries of fending off invasion, adapted from each of the styles of martial arts of the invaders. I learned that it was adapted by the Spetsnaz, the Russian special forces, as their style of fighting. And in the course of this research I learned about Vladimir Vasiliev, the man who brought the style to the mainstream. I was hooked after day one and felt a deep connection to style I was now training in.

It was not long after my first class that I learned that Vladimir was going to be holding a seminar in Tampa, just over a hours drive from my home, in April the following year. I had heard all the stories about Vlad's seminars, the long physical days, the endless number of strikes endured and the inestimable value placed on attending one. I immediately signed up and told my wife that we could bring my daughter and make a weekend of it in Tampa.

Over the months leading up to the seminar, David would do a phenomenal job of preparing us for what was ahead. A optional Saturday class was instituted, focusing on running, pushups and and strikes. Our regular Monday classes focused on fine tuning the fundamental breathing and movement techniques. It was truly an exciting time.

April came faster then any of us expected and before I knew it, I was standing in a room surrounded by Systema and martial arts practitioners from all over the world. There were marines from California, Brazilian Ju Jitsu artist from South Carolina, Aikido artist from south Florida and even Systema students from Istanbul. It was an amazing group of people and everyone had a smile on their faces.

The first night was a overview class lead by a senior Systema instructor. We learned new breathing techniques that focus on pushing the body outside of its element in regards to breath. We learned how to sense and move tension throughout the body. And we practiced a a few striking and self defense moves. We concluded the night by everyone introducing ourselves and stating what we enjoyed about the class. The positive vibe in that room was contagious and I could only imagine what was in store for us the following day.

The next morning I woke up and proceeded to the training facility early. When I arrived the gym was already bustling with activity. Groups of people were training, stretching and practicing breathing. Within the hour, the gym had well over a hundred people in it, everyone waiting for their opportunity to train with the master.

When Vlad arrived he wasted no time. Quickly he lead all of us to the center of the gym and laid out what was ahead for us over the next two days. From there we began performing some relaxation techniques to prepare our bodies for the day. Then into strikes, which we preformed until the break. It was after the break that I would experience something that would forever change me and deepen my appreciation for Systema.

When we returned from the break, we gathered us in the center of the gym. Vlad explained that we were going to do some training exercises and that they were going to be difficult. He said that when we began to feel like we could no longer perform the exercises to stop, really search ourselves and not to give up. All of us could do the exercises provided we look deeply inside ourselves. With that strong message, we spread out and get into a push up position.

Our next challenge was to do a twenty count push up. A twenty count push up is when you start off with your body upright, arms extended and then slowly begin to lower yourself to the count of twenty. At the 10 count you should be halfway down and all the way down at zero. The count then begins again and you slowly rise to the count of twenty. If you have never tried a push up this way I would urge you to do so. It is both a test of your physical abilities as well as your mental. The burning sensation and physical discomfort can become nearly unbearable. We had preformed these types of push ups before in class so when I heard Vlad say this was going to be the exercise I felt pretty confident that I could do it.

Then he added some additional steps. After the first twenty count push up we were to do continuous push ups until he called for a fifteen count push up which was then to be followed by continuous push ups again until Vlad called enough. As always in Systema these push ups were to be done on the knuckles. And off were were.

The count began and I slowly began to descend. Almost immediately I could feel the hardness of the gym floor meeting my knuckles. By 15 my hands were already sending messages to my brain. Flatten out your hands, sink faster, do anything other than what you are doing.

By ten the pain began to set into my triceps. I began to scan the room and many people had already flattened out their hands. I held firm and before I knew it we reached the bottom. As soon as the hit the bottom however the count began again and we were on our way up. I began to do burst-breathing, as David had taught us to do when the body was being pushed hard.

The pain was now making a continuous cycle from my hands, though my arms, across my shoulders and back into my hands. When we hit 20, fully extended, Vlad called out to begin doing continues push ups. It was sheer misery. Each push up felt like someone was closing a vice on my knuckles, each one felt like my triceps was going to simply give out.

Vlad then called to stop and our 15 count push up began. Again I scanned the room there were now more people on flat hands then on their knuckles. And many had simply stopped doing the push ups all together. My brain was like a train station, loud and chaotic. I wanted nothing more then to find some form of relief for the pain I was experiencing. Then I remembered what Vlad said , when we get to the point that we think we can no longer go on, search ourselves, dig deep. I remember I said "quiet" out loud. I focused on nothing other than the sound of Vlad's voice counting and my own breathing.

I closed my eyes and simply breathed through the pain. By the time the 15 count push up was over the pain had all but subsided. When the continuous push ups began I was able to do more then I had after the 20 count. It was as if there was a well of energy inside me that was overflowing. I felt invincible, I had done something that just moments ago I though I could not. When Vlad called stop I push out 5 more for good measure.

I found some things in those push ups that day. I learned that the mind is is truly more powerful than the body. I learned that sometimes when things get chaotic you just need to quiet your mind, breath and focus on what matters. And most important found that there are no limitations to what one can do if one truly is determined. When I am faced with a problem that it seems there is no overcoming I simply remember those push up and I find a way. I will remember that moment, that sense of accomplishment until the day I die.

These are lessons that I can use everyday of my life, these are lesson that help to develop my self.

We Need Purple Shirts

by

Christy LeDuc

1 out of every 6 American women has been the victim of an attempted or completed rape in her lifetime (14.8% completed rape; 2.8% attempted rape).

Approximately 2/3 of rapes were committed by someone known to the victim.[1]
73% of sexual assaults were perpetrated by a non-stranger.[1]
38% of rapists are a friend or acquaintance.[1]
28% are an intimate.[1]
7% are a relative.[1]

A 2005 study reported that 7% of partnered Canadian women experienced violence at the hands of a spouse between 1999 and 2004. Of these battered women, nearly one-quarter (23%) reported being beaten, choked, or threatened with a knife or gun. *(Family Violence in Canada: A Statistical Profile, 2005)*

Almost two years ago I found myself single again and realized I will be reentering the dating pool. Without going into detail lets just say I have my share of "jerks" in that department.

I had seen the announcements for the Systema class at the community center were I take yoga classes and had been thinking about going for a long time. My last experience in martial arts was in Tae Kwan Do, where after I made yellow belt. Those classes were basically an open season to beat the tar out of me (and others). Needless to say I didn't stay long.

One day Amy, my yoga instructor said she had gone to a Systema class but didn't like being the only woman so she talked me (OK it really wasn't that hard to do) into going with her to the next class. I showed and she didn't.

I was nervous walking in and had no idea what to expect since the class was made up of almost entirely men.
 I was not sure how I would be treated either. I think my biggest fear was being made fun of by my lack of experience, which includes such basics as, make a fist, punching, or how to fall without smacking my head on the ground.

Much to my surprise everyone in class has always shown me great patience and kindness and a willingness to teach me. I do believe that this attitude comes from the instructor and has had a trickle down effect to the rest of the class.

The surprising part for me is how Systema has become so much more to me than just a self-defense class. I still have not totally figured out why I need to be there other than I know I am very unhappy when I can't go. I have been going through a lot rough stuff the last year and I know that both the yoga and Systema have help keep me sane and slipping deeper into depression.

Another aspect has been overcoming fear. I am still surprised on how much of a punch I can take and the knowledge that I can survive taking it without long term damage.

Any women reading this, I will let you in on a secret. The first night I took strikes (I know you guys were being easy on me) my stomach felt like the worst menstrual cramps I had ever had. Yes it sucked but was easily survivable.

The biggest fear I have encountered in class is the choke holds, but this stands to reason as it is one of the reasons I came in the door in the first place. Over twenty-four years ago I had incident with an ex-boyfriend (yes, he was an ex at the time). We were both at a gathering of friends at a mutual friends house and he was being his usually pouty self and I was in no mood to talk to him. So I didn't.

One of the guests had to leave and we all went to walk him out to his car and say goodbye. I remember seeing my ex coming out of the house and walking towards me. I figured we would have another screaming match like a hundred time before. I was wrong. He grabbed me by the throat and picked me off of the ground. I remember my sheer terror at not knowing what to do or how to defend myself.

The next thing I knew I hit my head on the ground and I saw flashes of light, thinking that the cartoons were true – you do see stars when you hit you head hard. My next thought was I have to get up. I could not defend myself on the ground but I also couldn't get up to this day I am not sure if I was knocked out or to afraid to get up. I also remember how the tree limbs lit up against the streetlights. I learned later that he had intended to strangle me. He threw me to the ground because his best friend took a swing at him and he had to get rid of me to swing at him. The ex left after that.

Even after all these years my throat has tighten up and my head and back hurt where I hit the ground while I type this but fewer tears than I expected.

Whenever we do choke holds in class, the hardest thing for me is to not hear the fear. The only way I can describe it is this when I am being choked there are two sets of voices in my head.

The soft one tells me I am not in danger and I am still breathing and a screaming banshee voice of fear (which is very hard to ignore) and drowns out the first voice. I know I have made a lot of progress in this area, since the banshee voice isn't always as loud. The night we had my requested choke holds class, my insomnia lasted over a week. The last time the banshee fear screamed that loud a couple of weeks ago my insomnia only lasted one night. I realize this will probably be one of the hardest things for me to overcome. I have wondered how much my partners sense this fear in me and how they are affected by it.

David has talked about how we all bring different energies to the room, which I believe. I remember having the same instructor for two different classes in college and the personality of each class was completely different because each class had a different set of students. I believe my purpose there is to shake you out of your boxes by turning them upside down and shaking it until you fall out and hit your heads on the floor. You men in class do take it way too seriously at times. There needs to be more color and whimsy like purple "Powerpuff Girl" shirts.

Most importantly I am getting you all ready for the ensuing midget zombie apocalypse. When it happens you will be ready to defend yourselves or if they are basketball players zombies you can ask yourselves "What would Christy do to defend herself?" I know it sometimes freaks out my fellow students that I show so much glee in hurting them, I think this comes from the fact that in the female perspective. Making someone say "ow" is hurting them where as in the male perspective it is sending each other to the hospital. Or maybe I just am the only one to voice it out loud.

I jest of course, relating to the above. Systema has had a great impact on my personal life as I mentioned but also my work life.

How I have used Systema at work? The transfer of energy from me to an object has help save time on some tasks. Stomping Sentricon termite bait stations back into the ground my boss is amazed that I can stomp them back in especially the one he would have had to re-drill the holes.

Whether it is work or personal, I can say that this art is now a part of my life. In fact, the line which used to separate "life" and "Systema" is now gone!

50th Trip

by

David Orman

Tomorrow will mark my 50th trip to W. Palm Beach to train in Systema. 50 times, all but 2 or 3 done solo. 20,000 miles. 300 hours of long, lonely driving. 250 hours of hard, physical training, complete with bruises, swelling and other assorted colorful additions. Countless punches, defenses and mistakes.

50 trips to train with the best martial arts instructor I have ever had.

50 trips to train in the best martial art I have ever experienced.

I mentioned this to a few people and was subsequently bombarded with questions.

How did you do this? Why did you do this? What was it like? How did you deal with the 6 hours of driving and 5 hours of training, all in one day? Was it worth it? You did this for how many years now, without missing? How? Why? When? etc. etc.

Instead of answering directly, I relayed an old Taoist tale that fits the bill.

You know this one. Is the glass is half full or half empty?

For the optimist, it is half full.

For the pessimist, it is half empty.

For the accountant, the answer depends upon the exact number of molecules compared with the exact number of potential molecules needed to fill the glass. If over 50%, it is half full. If under, half empty.

For the Zen master, neither the glass, nor the water actually exist. They are simply temporary concepts of the mind which will eventually pass.

For the philosopher, the question points to a deeper mean, a symbolic representation of life itself.

For the Quantum Physicist, the glass is almost totally empty. So is the glass itself. If you look at both from a quantum perspective, both glass and water are comprised mainly of empty space.

For the environmentalist, they are more worried about the water and how to get rid of all of the toxins.

For the politician, it is half full and half empty so they will tax both.

For the Systema Practitioner. . . . he simply grabs the glass and drinks the water.

Life is meant to be experienced, not analyzed.

Want to know what it is like to commit to something deeply like Systema? Come join me on my next trip.

And the one after. And the one after that.

The 100th trip will be around the corner before we know it.

Just Looking for Something to Do

by

Thomas Moses

Of course, there is sarcasm behind my chosen title. The art of Systema is so much more than just something to do. The roots of my introduction, however, into Systema did have something to do with a mere curiosity. I suppose I could just as easily have joined the local adult basketball league. I couldn't be more satisfied with my decision.

In September of last year, I found myself 42, overweight (about 80 lbs.), out of shape (on high BP medication), and over stressed in a job with tremendous responsibility. With a family to support, I was feeling all of these pressures while possibly neglecting my own individualism. Was this textbook midlife crisis? Possibly. All I knew though was that I wanted an inherent change to steer my life in a better direction. I thought, at the very least, that joining either a gym or some type of organized athletics would be a wonderful start.

As I perused the City of Winter Garden's Recreation Department mailer, I came across the listing for Systema, Russian Martial Arts. The title alone seemed very unique, interesting. "The only class of its type in Central Florida." It certainly stirred my curiosity. Naturally, having never heard of it, I looked it up online. I checked it out on YouTube. Indeed it seemed very unique. I even came in one night and interrupted David's (my soon to be instructor) class to observe. As always, David humbly obliged and allowed me to observe a few minutes of the class.

I remember my first night. I could hardly complete some of the easier calisthenics. I couldn't balance on one leg. The Systema forms, movements, and practices seemed a little more manageable. By the end of class I was completely drenched in sweat. I notice no one else was. I also remember our last few minutes gathering in a circle to listen to a couple of thoughts on fear.

Congruent with my Systema training, I was also going to the gym and running 3 mile stints. So everything complimented each other as I lost weight, lowered my blood pressure, and gained endurance. These improvements helped me in Systema class as I was less worried about being out of breath and more able to concentrate on the movements.

I also loved the humility that accompanied the art. From friends and coworkers, I had always heard of the "black belt mills" and how they seemingly were more motivated by profit and the business aspect of signing up kids and their families to their respective martial arts schools. I saw none of these in Systema. Humility and mutual respect was imminent.

David and his students have always been approachable and receptive to questions and advice. They also are the first ones to say they're still learning the art. This openness to learning is one of the elements of Systema I find favorable.

I remember the first night we practiced strikes. I'm a big, fairly strong man and was nervous though. I'm not sure what gave me more apprehension, receiving a strike from David or striking my classmates. Of course, with appropriate breathing, the fears were unfounded. I remember the discussion following class that night; "If you can do this, imagine what else you can do."

This management of fear is an extremely important aspect of Systema philosophy that I've been able to incorporate into other aspects of my life. Our number one rule is "don't get hit," but there is much to be said about getting hit and taking it well, or, not being phased at all. I find it almost comical now that what was a tension filled night has evolved into a scenario where we all are always asking "can we do strikes tonight?"

Breathing. Another aspect of Systema I've incorporated into other aspects of my life. Not only do I try to practice "correct" breathing during Systema class, I also do it while I'm running, working out, or preparing for a meeting at work. I even use the breathing during meetings, when they tend to become contentious.

The Saturday outdoor training has been terrific. Although I was unable to attend the much anticipated seminar in Tampa recently, these outdoor sessions have been very enjoyable (and challenging).

Our Central Florida Systema group is unique. My

classmates are as different as can be, coming from completely different backgrounds and professions. We cover a spectrum of age ranges and ethnicity. Yet we all seem to be on the same page when it comes to openness and mutual respect. It's very good chemistry as it seems like we all learn from each other.

I still cannot believe there isn't a long waiting list to get into this class for it is a true goldmine. My friends, family, and coworkers surely must be tired of my discussions on Systema! Really, though, I try to take advantage of every chance to bring new students. I really can't foresee a scenario where I no longer attend Systema classes, so I hope they're always accessible. I hope this class, in particular, instructor and fellow students, is always there.

Pre-, During and Post-Training Nutrition

by

David Orman

We love the the training aspect; that is, learning from teachers who are masters of kick defense, punch defense, knife work, multiple opponents etc. For all of us, there is never enough time. For some though, there is never enough energy.

Whereas we may not be able to correct the time aspect, we can make dramatic improvements relating to energy. Here are some suggestions:

<u>Pre-Training</u>

There are a couple of keys when it comes to pre-training nutrition. Firstly, be sure the body's 2 major organs associated with energy production are strong and healthy. According to Natural Medicine principles, the Lungs and the Spleen are the organs that supply the body with energy.

The ideal food of the lungs is asparagus, particularly the tips. Also proper breathing – a MAJOR emphasis in Systema – is an absolute must.

The herb used to strengthen the lungs, as well as provide the body with "Qi" or energy is Astragalus. It is also an excellent immune booster.

For the spleen, foods that are yellow, brown and golden in color are considered ideal. Examples include pineapple, potato and yellow squash. On the flip side, sugar and dairy will weaken the spleen quicker than anything.

A great spleen tonic herb is Hyssop.

As a general guideline, the herb Rhodiolia is an excellent energy tonic. Extracted from the high mountains, Rhodiola helps prevent fatigue, and helps the body deal with the damaging effects of oxygen deprivation.

Perhaps the most famous of pre-training formulas involves the use of honey. Boil 100g of honey in a liter of water. If you live in colder weather, add cinnamon or ginger. If you live in warm weather, add mint. They will counter the external temperatures. Boil for 30 mines and sieve the infusion. Serve cold or hot, it is very tasty as well.

During Training

The simplest is the most effective. Keeping hydrated is the key during training as there is a direct correlation between dehydration and performance. Even mild dehydration – 1% of body – which would create a reduction in muscle performance by as much as 10%.

If training is in humid weather or longer than 90 minutes, a carbohydrate-based drink which contains electrolytes is recommended. I have used Clif or Hammer Electrolyte drinks during marathons for example, and found them excellent.

If a person is drinking a lot and still noting signs of dehydration, this is an indication of Trace Mineral deficiency. Add some liquid trace minerals or a trace mineral tablet during training and this issue will be easily corrected.

Post-Training

The 2 major keys with post-training are (1) removing inflammation from the body and (2) strengthening the Kidney energy.

In terms of the first, a post-training meal should consist of proteins and ideally, fish, as it is an excellent source of healthy fats and oils which clear inflammation from the system.

If one cannot consume fish, Pharmaceutical Grade Fish Oil* is the next best thing. Most health stores carry this and these gel caps are an excellent way to reduce inflammation.

Massage, re-hydration of course and the use of the amino acid L-Glutamine are also high useful. Glutamine in short, helps with muscle recovery and healing. This amino is also the most abundant one in our muscles. Levels are draining during intense, long workouts and must be replaced.

In terms of factor #2 (Kidney energy is considered the energy source for long term, endurance training per Natural Medicine principles), there is an herbal formula called *Shou Wu Chih* which features the herb *Polygoni Multifluri.* It is considered the major tonic for the kidney energy. Found at most health stores, it is an inexpensive, slightly bitter tasting liquid.

Of course, each person's system is different and ideal programs should be designed for each individual, based upon their needs, type of training and overall unique physiology. However, the above suggestions are the most common and safe.

Training in any art takes a great deal of dedication, time and effort. By optimizing the body before, during and after sessions, we give ourselves the greatest chance to improve our skills and master our art. And have a lot of fun in the process.

* NOT all fish oils are useful. To identify which ones are safe, place a gel cap in the freezer for 20 minutes.

Take it out and the gel cap should be pliable. If it is stiff and "rock-like," it is an indicator that toxins are present.

In my experience working with literally 1000's of patients over the years, Pharmaceutical Grade Fish oil, though more expensive is the only one consistently pure and free of toxins.

Old dog, New tricks

by

Edward Wiatrowski

I don't come from a martial arts background that many of the other people in my class do. This is all very new to me. My total martial art experience is about one and a half months of Tae Kwon Do or as like to call it " Dance Class." The only other fight training that I have is the the very basic hand to hand taught in the military.

I remember when I was a kid my friend Steve's older brother and my Dad took Judo. I thought that was the coolest thing ever. When they would get ready to go to training in their black uniforms, it made you wonder what kind of great things they were learning to do. Steve's older brother wasn't allowed to train with us younger boys, as he was in high school and we were in elementary school. Whenever his parents weren't home we would go out in the yard and "train" with him. He would throw and flip us around. It was great. Boys being boys.

When I was growing up there also wasn't MMA fighting – just boxing and the occasional Judo match, (and of course the ever popular Professional Wrestling). Karate was big. Bruce Lee was the man. Those great martial arts movies with the words never matched the mouths on the actors made you wonder how do they moved and did those things. It was somewhere in this time when the seeds were planted, so to speak.

Years later I joined the military and became a Combat Engineer. Part of our training was some basic hand to hand combat skills. I really liked it because it was straight foreword; that is, if you are presented with this you can do that. It was heavily technique oriented and though it had its place, I knew that if I was to pursue martial arts one day, a more free-flow approach would be needed. Little did I know.

Years later, and again my youngest son and I are watching a Tae Kwon Do demonstration at a local mall. My son said "I want to do that." Watching them brought me back to the days of old when I thought about Steve's Dad and older brother, my military training and the feeling of wanting to pursue this training again. As such I found myself answering my son with the phrase, "OK. . . and so do I." I think I was as surprised by the response and he was.

A few days later we were signed up Tae Kwon Do lessons. It didn't take long for me to realize that this isn't what I was looking for. I was looking for that instruction that was straight forward. I wanted to learn how to defend myself and my family, but I only felt like I was learning how to "dance." I gave it about as much of my time and attention that I could stand. My son however continued on for several more months and achieved several belts, Today, he remembers none of it. Maybe father does know best!

Again a few years later (seeing a pattern here) I heard of Systema but I was not at a point in my life which I could pursue it or even try it. Like I had said before, I am a husband and a father and my ultimate goal is to be there for my family.

While at work one day, I had a person come charging at me with a round end table like it was a Captain America shield. That situation resolved itself with little damage done to self and others, but it made me start to think about the self-defense issue and the safety of the people on my crew.

Two weeks later, I looked up Systema (again) and found a place not too far away. I started going to the class a few months ago, and I have to say " I like it." I really like it!

I feel it is what I'm looking for. I feel like I learn something useful every time I attend, not jazz hands, fake punch or fancy feet fancy kicking. The simplicity of it is where the power lies. I am starting to see how things come together and looking forward to getting a better grip on it and being able to attend some of the bigger seminars.

The group of people that I meet while at these classes are great, and I can't say enough about the instructor. How far will I take this? Only time will tell. But I have told my wife that I would like to go to Canada and train with Vlad.

This is a style of martial arts that I can get excited about.

Systema: A Life Changer

by

Craig Newton

I remember as a kid always being fascinated with martial arts. My brothers and I would fight with plastic ninja swords and jump around like the masked assassins. For some reason I never asked my parents to take me to learn martial arts. Maybe I was too shy, or lacked the confidence. Maybe I just wasn't that interested in learning martial arts.

That changed when I stumbled upon Systema.

I am a big fan of special forces, particularly British Special Air Service or S.A.S.. I watched S.A.S videos all the time. Along the similar videos list there were some about Spetsnaz. One of their hand to hand fighting styles, Systema really caught my attention because it was so different, so smooth, and at the time a lot of it seemed unbelievable. I thought it had to be legit if Spetsnaz really use it. After all, special forces don't have time to mess around with "mickey-mouse" stuff.

The striking videos with Mikhail Ryabko would look fake to most people. He would seem to just extend his arm and people would drop like flies.

Then there were the videos of Vladimir Vasiliev where he would take on multiple attackers and it looks like he's not even trying because he's so relaxed. It never occurred to me to look up if this was taught anywhere local though.

One weekend in April 2011, my wife and I were driving to a friend's party, when she started reading out loud the activity listing in the community newsletter we received in the mail.

All I was hearing though was "bla bla bla *Systema* bla bla". "Systema!?" I said, completely interrupting her.

She went into a little more detail about it - Russian style martial arts, times, location, etc. This was a sign. It was too coincidental that I recently stumbled upon Systema videos and then to find out it taught spitting distance from my house.

Upon returning home that afternoon, I went on the computer and looked it up. I found out there's probably about a hundred people in the country certified to teach it and only a handful in Florida. This is too good to pass up. Some higher power is trying to spoon feed me a big opportunity.

The following Monday I show up for my first class, a little nervous not knowing what to expect. If I remember correctly I was the first one there. As soon as I met David Orman any nervousness went completely out the window. He just came across straight away as being a nice, easy going guy. He almost seemed surprised to see me, almost humble I should say. Apparently I wasn't the only one who saw the sign from a higher power as there were a few other first-timers that class.

The class size doubled overnight as I later learned there were only a few regulars before then. I have even joked with David that he did some "Systema rain dance" that night.

One of the things that surprised me the most was how laid-back and informal the class is. I think that's one of the great things about this class. It feels like there's no pressure to perform. Everyone is just having fun learning this amazing art. It's like a paradox - people having fun learning an art that potentially can cause great harm or even death to another human being.

The energy is just so positive. There have been several times I have attended class being a bit tired, stressed about work, or even an emotional wreck. But after all those classes, I felt a million times better. They say martial arts has hidden benefits and it's the truth! In fact, it is a truth that is rarely even mentioned.

Going back to my first class, I remember how excited I was afterward. I couldn't wait until next class, and I told myself I was taking a punch next time. You see, at the end of the first class David asked if anyone wanted to feel the Systema strike. After watching Mikhail videos you can understand why I didn't volunteer. I believe one or two people took strikes.

After watching them take hits I felt a little more comfortable about it. I could see it was not David's intention to hurt anyone, or give them more than they can handle. I did eventually get my strike, and that's the moment I became a believer. Thump! "Breathe! Breathe!"

I could feel the energy go straight through my body almost in slow motion, and it felt like it was pulling out my guts with it. It lingered for a few seconds and as I focused on breathing it quickly went away.

 I felt like a new man, like I conquered a fear. The difficult thing for me taking strikes thereafter was relaxing and not trying to react. It's very unnatural to stand relaxed with your eyes open while a fist is coming at your stomach and not tighten up. Taking strikes is only half of it though.

Giving strikes proved to be a bit of a challenge as well. You would think hitting someone is one of the most basic, neanderthal things to do but as with anything everything in this art, there is the Systema way.

The best strikes I have done felt to me to be the weakest. It still boggles me how little effort it takes for a hard strike when done properly. It's actually hard for me to swallow. At this point I'm not even sure I would pull it off in a real self defense encounter, something I hope never to be involved in.

After doing a few classes I did start to feel like a little tougher, stronger and more confident that I could handle myself. A little over a year of classes now and I actually, strangely enough, feel less confident in some ways. It sounds crazy but the more I learn and the more drills we do, the more I'm starting to realize how much I really don't know.

We are starting to be more unpredictable with each other, and working at faster speeds but still a fraction of a real fight speed. It keeps getting more and more challenging. I have great respect for anyone who has trained in any art for years and years. I have started to realize that you can never truly master an art, only get better.

I remember our first Saturday training with David Merrell, an instructor from W. Palm Beach. I believe he was the first American to be trained by Vladimir and has around 20 years experience. It was another taste of what experience and skill level looks like.

I thought our instructor was a bad-ass, and I still do, but it seemed he couldn't touch Mr. Merrell by his own admisssion. Then I start thinking Mr. Merrell probably wouldn't stand a chance against Vladimir, and Vladimir would probably tell you Mikhail is better than him. No matter how good you are, there's always someone better.

The training with Mr. Merrell ended that day with more questions then answers. I suppose that's a good thing. If I never have questions then I'm not learning enough.

April 2012 was Vlad's seminar in Tampa. The first and hopefully not the last time meeting the legend.

There had to be over a hundred people there. Laying on the floor of the USF gym doing breathing and muscle tension exercises, struggling at first to understand Vlad's strong Russian accent, it was a surreal experience for me. Everyone was sitting in a circle around him, just inches from him while he demonstrated what he does best.

His movement has to be seen in person to be believed, as the YouTube videos do not do it justice. He didn't hold back either. Some of the guys that volunteered took a good beating. Those guys were like rock stars, in the sense that everyone gave them props for taking strikes.

I also enjoyed training with other people from different regions and skill levels. There were some really skilled people there and overall a lot of good people.

Vlad was such a humble guy and was more than happy to answer questions and take pictures. He's not what most people would expect either. If someone described his ability you would draw a picture in your mind of this seven foot tall guy that fights tigers and eats lions. The reality is he doesn't eat lions and is not seven foot tall. I'm sure he could still take down a tiger though he would be more apt to help one. Some people wear Superman pajamas. Superman wears Vladimir pajamas. You get the idea.

If I only ever get to a fraction of Vlad's skill level I'll be happy with that. It's a long road ahead. I've only been training Systema a little over a year now, and

I don't plan on ever stopping. It has changed my life for the better. Even if I never have to use my training in a real situation, I'm okay with that. The whole experience is worth it to me. The confidence I have built, the fear I have overcome, and the friends I have made have been dramatic.

Thanks to my new friends, or should I say comrades, for we share the same goals and help each other conquer the same fears. Special thanks to my instructor David Orman, for he has opened a door for me. I can only dream of giving back what Systema has done for me.

Systema: A Personal Experience

by

Gary Parody

I have experienced several martial arts first hand and have read and/or heard about numerous others. When it came to Systema- not word one!

Other than Sambo, I had no knowledge of Russia even having a martial arts "system." While reading the paper, I noticed a small blurb about Systema. Sysema in this area? Having a Russian martial art offered in the relatively small town of Winter Garden was rather amazing. And exciting!

Needless to say my curiosity was piqued. Not knowing what to expect, I decided to check it out. First I went to to websites then to YouTube clips of course, trying to get an idea of what this RMA is all about.

The sites and clips provide some idea, albeit limited ones, of what this art is about. It was beneficial to see some clips, but there is nothing - I mean nothing like experiencing Systema for yourself.

Going to my first class, I really had no idea of what to expect. Now, after 3 years of training, I can say it truly has changed all my perspective of my previous training. There are common threads, but Systema approaches martial arts in its own unigue way.

For the most part , it turns everything upside down so to speak.

One of the first things you realize is, so much of what you are used to is thrown out the window. There are no stances, no katas and no techniques. No techniques in martial arts? The concept was hard to even grasp.

I think all martial arts in general are just fascinating. Aside from one my other favorites, Arnis, this has to be one of the most interesting, unique, practical, flowing, devastating art I have come across. It uses the body in a non –traditional way. I would describe it as a natural, flowing, seemingly effortless way. The emphasis on being tension free. Breathing goes to another level, never before experienced in any martial art. This allows for the absence of memorized patterns and the freedom to naturally deal with the opponent(s). By eliminating the tension, strikes become incredibly powerful. There is a term used that their strikes are "heavy". That is an understatement!!!

One of the best experiences though has been meeting some incredible people. Many different types, different ages, sizes, and backgrounds all coming together to learn this martial art. The ability to leave the ego out, the willingness to try something different that is so outside the comport zone are also some of the great experiences I have had. It has been amazing how the art can bring people together, even though you may be unloading with strikes to one another!

I believe it has had such an impact on me

personally which goes beyond martial arts. It truly carries over and reaches out to other areas of my life. Many martial arts emphasize building character, but Systema and our school's focus on" life lessons" without a doubt, has pushed me in such a positive impact in my life. I have done my best to apply these lessons with family, work and self. What I have learned in training as it applies to everyday life, has been some of the most beneficial and powerful aspects.

What could be any better than learning an amazing martial art and growing as a person?!

I wonder what's next!?

Teaching Titles in Systema
by
David Orman

In Japanese, the term is "Sensei."

In Chinese, it is "Sifu."

In Russian arts including Systema, it is. . . . it is. . . .what is it?

This was the question posed to my Russian friends who are long term practitioners of Systema and other arts and residents of various cities in Russia. Russians, born and raised, practicing Russian arts. In other words, I went right to the source.

Their answer to the question "Is there a title for a Russian Martial Arts instructor?" was most interesting.

To quote exactly, *"No, and what for? The Sensei in the East is the whole cult, it both culture and tradition. In Russia there is no such understanding as martial* **art.** *It is more skill, ability or tradition. It is good to be able to fight in Russia always was norm."*

In other words (filtering the translation), it is a way of life more than a separate entity. As such, titles only get in the way. They feed the ego where as training feeds the body, mind and Spirit. "*No and what for?*" pretty much addresses all.

I find this a very useful approach in my personal quest in Systema. I learn so much from my teachers and also volumes from my students. In fact, the line between teacher and student is non-existent. Whether expert or beginner, we are all on the same never ending, ever intriguing path.

This fascinating art of Systema just keeps getting more and more interesting.

Proper Breathing and the Impact on My Life

by

Mark C. Henderson

The Russian martial art, Systema, emphasizes breath work, striking, knife and gun defense, defense from multiple attackers, floor movement, wrestling, joint locks, defense with clothes, you name it, the list goes on.

Now, I am not a martial arts expert, hold no dan ranks, and have limited experience. However, when I watch tapes, I see that the masters work with grace and fluidity, attributing it to breathing properly and learning how to control their fear... I want to be like them!

Breathing itself is a seemingly simple task; however when I feel fear, I hold my breath, which roots me in place. If I don't breathe, I can't move! So, to mitigate fear, taking strikes, breath work and movement are core. I feel that:

a) sometimes with stress it is difficult to simply remember to breathe and
b) prior to Systema training, I never did breath work, except in an occasional yoga class. So this is a huge learning experience for me.

Systema is not a soft, non contact art by any

means. I learned the hard way that getting hit and feeling a connection is fundamental.

Before I started I thought that the best way to take a punch was to "steel" yourself, and bounce back the shot with your body. When I tried to "get tough" I was dropped, really fast. The punches hurt and the pain lingered inside my body. I wanted to keel over and die on the spot - until I finally made the connection that it is easier to take strikes if you are relaxed, go with the hit, and maintain your breathing pattern and posture. Exactly what Systema preaches in life. I feel a little more confident taking strikes now, but I have a long way to go.

My favorite experience so far was the camp featuring Vladimir Vasiliev in Tampa. This guy is real. I was both very excited and nervous going to camp. Vladimir showed me how little force is needed to defend an attack. He worked with me like a phantom! I remember not being able to tell where his hand and my wrist separated. His grip was so light, I could barely tell that he was holding me, but he was able to easily move me in any direction when I came in to attack. When he hit me, it felt like a shock wave!! I remember holding my jaw gaping "Whoa" and he grinned and said, "Good connection?" and started working with someone else.

I am happy being part of Central Florida Systema. I

felt welcome from day one. In my short time there I feel I have made many friends and learned a lot about myself.

I've noticed that the more I do breath work, the more I catch myself holding my breath. After I practice, I feel more alive!! Also, more alert, free from stress. Calm.

Many aspects of my life have improved. I feel a little more comfortable talking with people. Could it be so simple that the absence of proper breathing is the major cause of discord in society?

I'm working on the basics and will continue to do so. It's been an incredible experience.

My Venture Into Systema

by

Neal Hamner

I found my way into the world of Systema quite by accident, somewhat by chance, but mostly I believe because of destiny. I have always been interested in firearms and found myself watching a program on the History Channel one Saturday afternoon, about the most famous firearms in history. Of course one of my personal favorites, the AK-47, was featured and the program went on to elaborate on its origins, the AK's impact on modern warfare, and the groups and organizations that readily employ the rifle's use.

One of the groups was the Spetsnaz and the History Channel did a 30 second blurb on the elite special forces group and their use of the almost "indefensible" martial art known as Systema. I was instantly intrigued but soon forgot about it, thinking I would probably never see or hear the term again. As fate would have it though, that was not the case at all.

A few weeks later my wife and I were having breakfast at a local establishment and I saw a flyer advertising local Systema classes. I could not believe it! I immediately took down all the information and joined the school a few days later.

There were only three of us initially, but as time went on, it grew and grew. Now we are a large group that have truly grown into something very special.

I think I am going on three years now and have truly enjoyed every minute of it. I also met a great human being, David Orman, who would quickly become not only my trainer and instructor, but, more importantly, my friend.

Why Did You Wait?

By

David Orman

**Dedicated to all want-to-be Systema practitioners who are waiting to start their training.

Life goes by just so fast.

It seems like yesterday, I turned 20. Having just finished college, I wanted to take a couple of weeks off and do some traveling. Parts of California seemed to be calling my name but I decided I would wait, despite having the opportunity. It seemed finding work and saving the monies I had, would be a more practical strategy. Ironically, I never did manage to get to see what I wanted.

It seems like yesterday, I turned 30 and saw a woman I wanted to date. She seemed to have everything I ever wanted – looks, personality, great energy. I was going to ask her out but I decided to wait. It wasn't the right time as I was preparing to get a new job and may be moving. Turns out, I did not move, nor get the job. Nor did I ask her out, but I did get to meet her. She eventually became my best friend's wife.

It seems like yesterday, I turned 40 and decided to finally start a family. Having been married a few years, I thought I would enjoy family life. But I decided to wait. We had not moved into the ideal house and a few other factors were not quite right.

A couple of years later, we did get that perfect house. By then, the biological clock has gone past the stroke of midnight and children were out of the question.

It seems like yesterday, I turned 50 and wanted to finally start my own business. I had been in the same job for almost 30 years and though it had the illusion of security, it was far from rewarding. In fact, it was just a job. A pay check. The passion that existed, if it ever existed, was long gone. What replaced it was a tedious 9-5 and a bimonthly pay check. I decided to wait to start the business however. I hung in with the job this long and could take early retirement in another 5 years. Then I will start the business. So I waited. Unfortunately, by then, my unique business which I would have absolutely loved, opened up down the street. Someone else had the same idea and made a *not-so-small* fortune doing it.

It seems like yesterday, I turned 60 and decided to retire. At least now I could finally start to live. At least now, I could finally do the things that I had put off or travel to the sights of my dreams. I decided to wait however. The economy was in a steep downturn and I was worried about my future. What if one of us got sick? Also the roof was looking a little roughed up. Dreams could always wait. The roof needed fixing soon.

It seems like yesterday, I turned 70 and I slowed down quite a bit. I wanted to go visit some friends and family that I had not seen in a while. Not sure when I would see them again. But I decided to wait. Gas prices were high and I really did not like driving the distance. Granted it was only 50 miles but Christmas was only 5 months away anyway. We would probably see each other then.

It seems like yesterday, Christmas came but I was too sick to see anyone. I wanted to say my last goodbyes but it was the holiday season so I decided to wait. Once the holidays were over, things would settle a bit and then we would have time to talk and catch up with family and friends.

It seems like yesterday, I died. In fact, it was yesterday.

I was told by the angels I would be seeing God in 3 days, so I decided to prepare for my last judgment. I looked at my life and realized I had made countless mistakes and careless errors. I hoped God would understand, but just in case I wrote down as many excuses, explanations, rationalization, alibis, justification and revisions as I would muster. I even threw in some glorious stories, whitewashing and *song and dances*. When all of these were exhausted, I could simply ask for forgiveness and then take my medicine appropriately.

The third day came and I met God. He was much smaller than I pictured, and after all these years, still no gray hair.

The most imposing thing was the loving aura and despite being in heaven, had an indescribably down-to-earth demeanor.

I was sweating the way I would sweat during one of my marathons that I imaged doing, but never got around to running. My heart was beating uncontrollably. I knew my myriad of excuses and stories was a pathetic scheme, unworthy of presenting to a human yet alone the One. Nonetheless I clutched my pages and pages of notes the way a baby chimp clutches her mother.

Then something strange happened. There was no judgment. No punishment. There was just love, a smile and one simple question:

"Why did you wait?"

Judgment was not needed. I had already judged the situations when I lived on Earth – judged instead of listened to His Voice whispering "stop waiting and go for it."

I had already punished myself, so no punishment was needed. I missed out on people, places and opportunities that would have make an OK life, a glorious one. A gray life into one brimming with color and effervescence.

I was simply left with the question, *"Why did you wait?"*

The pain of trying to answer the question must have done it. I awoke to sweat soaked bed sheets, a pounding heart and a clock reading 3:09am. What a horrible nightmare.

I immediately got out of bed, put on my gear and started training. It was 3:30 in the morning, hot and raining but so what. I wasn't waiting for dawn. I wasn't waiting for the rain to stop. I wasn't waiting for it to cool down. I wasn't waiting for my friends to join me.

In fact, I am never going to wait again.

Special Note

For those looking for more information, please go to **CFLSystema.wordpress.com**.

You can also visit one of our classes at:

Jesse Brock Center
310 N. Dillard St.
Winter Garden, FL 34787
407 810 2171

David Orman, Instructor
david.orman@yahoo.com

Printed in Great Britain
by Amazon